MARK OESTREICHER

LEADING WITHOUT POWER

Every once in a while Christian leaders need a voice like Marko's to jolt them back to the reality that how they lead should be a reflection of what they believe about Jesus. It's ironic. Since Jesus was all-powerful, he could have easily leveraged his power to influence a generation. But he didn't. Instead he chose to lead from a perspective of love and empathy. *Leading Without Power* challenges every leader to turn up the humility and turn down the ego if they hope to have lasting influence with this generation.

Reggie Joiner I @reggiejoiner
Founder and CEO of Orange
Author of *Lead Small*

There's a time and a place in every person's life and ministry when they will choose how they will lead. It's my hope and prayer that more pastors and ministry leaders would see the power that is theirs to hurt or to heal. Marko has written a book that describes much of what we long to see and gives us a place to begin as we make these subtle yet empowering shifts together. This one is a must read.

Brooklyn Lindsey I @brooklynlindsey
Justice Advocate, Nazarene Youth International
Author of *A Parent's Guide to Understanding Teenage Girls*

I have had the privilege of watching first-hand the profound impact Marko has in the groups he works with. With no positional power, his leadership invites transformation, freedom, and empowerment of those he serves. In *Leading Without Power*, we get a peek into the process that has made such a difference in the lives of so many in ministry.

Marko's cohort work through The Youth Cartel has been an ideal laboratory for *Leading Without Power*, making this one of the most "real" leadership books you will ever read.

Mark DeVries | @markdevriesyma
Founder of Ministry Architects and Permissionary
at Ministry Incubators
Author of *Sustainable Youth Ministry*

Sometimes in the church, we find a leadership book that tweaks our perspective on leadership and catches us up to the reality of leading in today's world. That's what Mark Oestreicher has done with *Leading Without Power*. It's not the usual leadership book, because it's not theoretical. It's 100% immersed in first-hand experience leading current generations. Every leader should go through this and ask some great questions about what leading looks like right now. It's so incredibly helpful, not only for youth leaders but all leaders.

Dan Kimball | @dankimball
Pastor of Mission & Leadership, Vintage Faith Church
Author of *They Like Jesus But Not the Church*

Leading Without Power
9 Paths Toward Non-Coercive Ministry Leadership

By Mark Oestreicher

THE YOUTH CARTEL

Leading Without Power
Copyright © 2017 by Mark Oestreicher

Publisher: Mark Oestreicher
Managing Editor: Tamara Rice
Cover Design: Adam McLane
Layout: Adam McLane
Creative Director: Gideon

ISBN-13: 978-1-942145-29-5
ISBN-10: 1-942145-29-2

The Youth Cartel, LLC
www.theyouthcartel.com
Email: info@theyouthcartel.com
Born in San Diego

Printed in the U.S.A.

CONTENTS

INTRODUCTION
ORGIN (AND A SEMANTIC ACKNOWLEDGEMENT)

I like power.

As I've grown older, I long to see this inclination decrease and be replaced by humility and other traits that are more in alignment with Jesus. And I've seen God do a wonderful work of transformation in my life over the last two decades.

Part of the tension is that the exercising of power has—while often creating problems and doing harm—brought plenty of benefits to my life.

I have a friend who traveled as a youth speaker and was known for his energetic, passionate, and even manic presentation style. Then he was diagnosed as bipolar and put on meds. The meds were absolutely needed and helped him survive. But they also shaved off his powerful manic moments, which he'd come to rely on when on stage speaking to teenagers. He deeply struggled with how to re-imagine his presentation style if he couldn't tap into that manic frenzy that people responded to so positively.

I understand that. I long to be a leader who influences people toward the Kingdom of God, and I increasingly long to do that without the exercising of coercive or manipulative power. But those tools in my leadership tool belt—the coercive and manipulative set—used to work really well for me (most of the time).

I got promoted (many times) because of the powerful way I led.

I was given meaningful responsibilities.

I was praised.

At one church, I was hired as the junior high pastor and two months later, promoted to oversee junior high through college ministry. And when that church's senior pastor imploded four months later, I was selected as one of a small team of this large church's staff to give interim leadership to the church and input to the church board.

The two men leading this effort sat me down and told me very specifically why they were choosing me for this responsibility and honor (these are actual words): "You are a powerful leader. And your lack of mercy is the strength of your leadership."

Needless to say, I had some lessons to unlearn in future years.

About 20 years ago now, I began to see the problems with this style of leadership. Primarily this was due to being increasingly uncomfortable with how much damage I occasionally wrought in the lives of people I cared about, even when the overall ministry results would have been considered a win. I sought out mentors to help me grow. I read books. I prayed. I asked forgiveness.

Of course, this wasn't an overnight change, and it's unquestionably an ongoing project. But I can look back over these past two decades and see significant growth: the old me giving way to a new, transformed me.

I still like power. But I can now easily recognize that natural inclination (and the accompanying feelings, motivations, and not-yet-taken actions). And I can choose a different path, with different choices. I can lead with influence but not coercion or manipulation.

THE NEXUS OF THIS BOOK

Early in this process of change, I picked up a book by noted leadership guru Max De Pree. I had read one of his earlier excellent books on leadership, either Leadership Jazz or Leadership Is an Art (both still worthy reads), and was instantly intrigued by the title of this small third book: Leading Without Power: Finding Hope in Serving Community.[1]

Honestly, it's not De Pree's best book, more of a collection of short essays on leadership in the nonprofit world, where "customers" aren't paying for a product and much of the work is done through volunteers. There are some helpful nuggets in the book, to be sure. But the title itself is what messed with my head. And for 20 years now, I've been rolling those three words around, experimenting and playing with what they might look like.

That's what lead to this small book. With apologies (and thanks) to De Pree, I'm just using the same title, since they are the words that have guided me through years of developing this material, even though the content you'll read here is 100% different from De

Pree's and of my own creation (as is the subtitle).

I'd be very happy if the title of any of my books results in people ruminating on an idea for 20 years.

A SEMANTIC ACKNOWLEDGEMENT

I'll just get this on the table right now: One could easily argue that this entire book is a semantic game, at least when connected with its fairly bold title. Leadership of *any sort* has power inextricably woven into it. In a sense, there can be no such thing as "leading without power." If leadership is actually occurring, power plays a role, even if that leadership is unintentional.

My 18-year-old son texted me from college. He asked if I had heard the new release by a musician in a genre my son knows I normally don't choose. In a sense, it was an absurd question, and he had to have known the answer would be no. Whether he knew he was doing this or not, he was certainly hoping I would listen to the album and decide I liked it enough to buy it, which (since my son and I share an iTunes account) would mean he would have the album also.

Music is a connection point for my son and me and has provided many memories (particularly of attending concerts together) and conversations. Our musical tastes overlap at roughly 80%, and I enjoy our dialogue about the 20% as much as I enjoy the dialogue about the overlap.

I texted him back, though, and told him that I'd listened to a few songs on the album and, while I respected the work, didn't think it was likely that I would purchase it. He responded with "Cool," and that was that.

Except: I gave it a second listen. And a third and fourth. And the album really grew on me. There was genius in it and a level of creativity and genre-rejection that was uncommon.

So, I bought it and ended up listening to it nonstop, while I worked, for the next four days.

I chose this example here because of its inconse-quential nature. Max didn't set out to lead me. At best, he wanted to share with me something he found interesting. At worst, he was hoping I'd buy the album so he didn't have to.

But in that experience, Max was absolutely leading me. And, I would be flat-out denying the definition of power if I tried to explain away this exchange saying that Max's leadership of me wasn't imbedded with power. There's no leadership without power. That is true when it's obvious. And that is true when it's not obvious, or when the exercising of leadership is unintentional.

With that said, allow me a semantic maneuver. While what I've just written about power is true, most of us don't think of power (particularly when connected to leadership) with that framing. Most of us think of power in leadership to mean *coercive, top-down, authoritative power.*

This sort of power, I suggest (with no research or footnotes), is the dominant practice of leadership in most organizational leadership (business, civic/political, nonprofit, church). It's what we're accustomed to. It's what we expect.

Even if organizational leadership is good and pure and lovely (and not overly coercive or manipulative), it's still normally imbued with assumptions about the leader's position, authority, and ability to say yes or no.

This is the reality—our collective understanding of the function of leadership as hierarchical and authoritative—that I hope to side-swipe by suggesting that ministry leadership should be marked by leading *without* power.

And it's this understanding of the function of leadership

that I hope to see continually decreasing in my own leadership.

1
REFRAMING POWER IN CHRISTIAN LEADERSHIP

I'd love you to at least briefly reflect on some questions as we jump in:

- *In what ways do I have power in my role?*
- *In what ways do I lack power?*

I don't know your ministry role. You might be a senior pastor, a business leader who serves on a church board, a youth worker (my people), paid employee or volunteer, a staff person in a missions or parachurch ministry organization, or in one of thousands of other ministry roles.

And I don't know your context. It might be rigidly

hierarchical or gloriously flat and egalitarian (and chaotic!). Most likely, it's a mixture, somewhere in-between those extremes.

But whether you are paid or volunteer, you absolutely have power in your ministry role. You make decisions, and carry out plans, and influence people.

Let me use two of my current roles as an example.

After years of church employment (in roles from junior high pastor to executive pastor), I moved to an organization called Youth Specialties, which trained and provided resources for church youth workers. I spent a few years as the publisher and another eight as the president. After some difficult upheaval in 2009, I launched out on my own, founding The Youth Cartel, a similar-but-not-similar organization that provides resources and coaching for church youth workers.

The Youth Cartel (the publisher of this book you're reading!) is a tiny group of revolutionaries obsessed with both building up youth workers and upsetting apple carts.

In my role as a partner at The Youth Cartel, I'm a sort-of employee (technically, I'm a contractor, as are many ministers). And I have sort-of employees (the people who work with and for us are extremely "free range"). We don't have an office, and I work from home.

But I'm leading as much or more than I ever have. I might not be creating employee policies or doing much hiring and firing. But I'm actively speaking into the lives of hundreds of youth workers through our coaching program and other initiatives.

A fun little example from, as I write this, the past two days:

Two days ago, I was in San Jose, California, speaking to a small group of about 25 Southern Baptist youth workers (mostly volunteers, some paid). I trained them on a variety of subjects, but spent time at one point talking about the isolation of teenagers in our culture and our churches and how it's counter-productive to their faith formation.

I received an email from a woman who attended that training, Carmen, asking me if I would share my notes, as she was heading into an interview to be considered for the role of part-time youth director at her church and wanted to review some things she hadn't written down. Of course, I'd gladly shared my notes with her.

Yesterday she sent this email:

Thank you so much for the notes! I was actually able to use so much of what I learned from you during my interview in front of my church council. I was asked a question about the youth and church services.

Man 1: "Why don't the youth group attend church service?"

Me: "Well it's probably because we've isolated them. We just encourage them to come to youth group on Wednesdays in the back building. Of the 25 kids in youth group, two of them play and sing in the worship team, but we haven't given the others any responsibility or roles they could play. Or even let them know we want them at Sunday services."

Man 2: "I agree with her. How many of us have gone on Wednesday night to invite the kids or to even remind them we have services on Sunday? I know I haven't, and I bet a lot of you in here haven't either."

To make a long story short, I'm officially the youth director of First Baptist! The vote was unanimous.

Thanks again for sharing your truths and knowl-edge!

Really, that little email made my day.

And: There is no arrogance in acknowledging that I *led* Carmen and that some sort of power was involved.

My other primary ministry role these days is being a junior high volunteer at my church. I'm not paid staff at my church but have attended there (and been a junior high volunteer) for 18 years. These days, my primary involvement with our junior high ministry is as a small group leader.

Three weeks ago, I started a new small group with a dozen seventh grade boys and two co-leaders. The first two weeks were absolute chaos, and I knew in my gut that it was going to be near impossible to accomplish much with such a large group of squirrels, even with three adult leaders.

So, at our third meeting, our small group started out together to set up our topic (which was "stress and worry"), then broke into three mini-groups of four boys and one leader each. This changed everything. I had the single-most-squirrelly guy in my mini-group; and while he still rolled around (literally) and fiddled with things and never stopped moving, he actually had some amazingly insightful things to add to our conversation.

One of the other guys in my mini-group, Alex, called out to me as I was walking across the church parking lot en route to my car to head home. He wanted me to meet his mom.

Now, let's state the obvious: I'm not employed at my church. And we have a full-time junior high pastor I serve under. I did not choose who was going to be in my small group, or what night we meet on, or where our group meets, or any one of a hundred other important leadership decisions and actions. But am I leading and exercising power? Undeniably, both in decisions like the format change and apparently in relationships.

REFRAMING POWER

What kind of power do we see Jesus exercise in his leadership?

Jesus' leadership and exercising of power challenges me. He's certainly not powerless. Of course, Jesus possessed (and possesses) limitless power.

But I would contend that we never once see Jesus

use coercive power, except when he's confronting demons. Even the single instance we see of big-time feistiness—when Jesus flips over tables in the temple courtyard, surely creating a massive moment of awkward tension—is ultimately not coercive, as he wasn't viewed as someone with authority to tell anyone other than his followers what to do. He would have merely been seen as an angry crazy man disrupting the tried-and-true practices of moneychangers and animal offering salespeople (who, I'm sure, had nicely crafted mission statements about how they were assisting in the spiritual work of a sacred space).

Since Jesus had unlimited power, the question shifts from quantity to quality; or, the question shifts from *if* one can exercise power to *how* one exercises power. And, what form that power takes.

I'm sure there are a hundred more forms, but here's a short list of power forms—good, bad, and indifferent:

- Coercion
- Manipulation
- Positional authority
- Officially dispensing rewards and punishment
- Signing paychecks

- Ability to control
- Personality
- Ideation
- Encouragement
- Truth-telling
- Serving
- Facilitation

LEVEL 5 LEADERSHIP

In 2001, noted business author Jim Collins published his most widely read book, *Good to Great*.[2] The book is a brilliant, research-based explanation of why some organizations experience protracted seasons of significant growth, while others follow a more predictable series of growth seasons interrupted by seasons of struggle.

There are dozens of important insights in this book for ministry leaders, and these have been widely discussed in other books and articles and at ministry conferences.

But one aspect of Collins' research particularly haunted me: his notion of "Level 5 Leadership."[3] Collins found that the best organizations (based on a research metric of sustained growth over a long period of time) are led by Level 5 Leaders. It's not a surprising idea that great organizations would have great leaders. But even Collins was surprised by the counter-cultural traits of this type of leader.

The Level 5 Leader is one who, according to Collins, possesses a "paradoxical blend of personal humility and professional will."[4]

Collins acknowledges that this sort of leader is very rare and that most leaders tend to have high will tethered to ego, or humility coupled with lower expectations and drive. Collins also suggests that one cannot *grow* into being a Level 5 Leader, that these rare leaders have this combination of humility and will deep within them long before they rise to a position of influence. But I deeply want Collins to be wrong in this assumption. My opposition to his "born this way" stance is first based in my longing, my aspiration, to embrace humility while retaining my natural tendency toward will power. Additionally, I can't quite accept Collins' assertion at a theological level: I firmly believe (and have experienced) that God passionately wants to transform me into the likeness of Jesus and that the only true roadblock is my own resistance.

It would be, in its very nature, self-evidently untrue for

anyone (myself included) to declare oneself a Level 5 Leader. And I am still far from my goal. But I'm leaning in, and I'm learning, and I've seen progress in my 20-year spiritual quest.

At the end of the day, isn't that description of a Level 5 Leader a pretty good description of Jesus' leadership and use of power?

Personal humility:

> *[Jesus,] who, being in very nature God, did not consider equality with God something to be used to his own advantage; rather, he made himself nothing by taking the very nature of a servant, being made in human likeness. And being found in appearance as a man, he humbled himself by becoming obedient to death—even death on a cross!*[5]

And professional will:

> *For I have come down from heaven not to do my will but to do the will of him who sent me.*[6]

Unfortunately this is, all too often, not the approach to power we see in most churches (or other places of leadership, to be fair).

The largest portion of my work these days is leading one of The Youth Cartel's programs called the Youth Ministry Coaching Program. This is a yearlong whole-life leadership development program for church youth workers. While we talk about youth ministry, our intentional outcomes aren't really focused on the pragmatics of youth ministry. Instead, we've found that healthy, growing youth workers tend to lead healthy, growing youth ministries. To that end, we focus on growing in self-knowledge, learning to lead from values, understanding and leading change, and thinking more deeply.

In the context of leading these cohorts (we put 10 youth workers in a cohort for this yearlong journey of growth), I've had the privilege of going *way past* superficial with hundreds of youth workers. They end up sharing their deepest fears and hopes, their pain and challenges.

This deep and honest look into the real lives of real youth workers has provided me many insights. But not the least of these realities is how jacked up leadership is in the majority of churches. Sure, there are plenty of wonderful exceptions to this. But over and over and over again, I see patterns of power being abused, manipulation, coercion, dishonesty, and pettiness borne out of insecurity. It's discouraging at times and regularly causes me to pray for the church and reaffirm my belief that the church is the bride of Christ. I regularly marvel that the love of Jesus would choose *this* bride.

A PROPOSAL

This book is anchored in this proposal: *Power-based leadership has no place in the church.*

I believe that at a theological level. But I have also seen it at a pragmatic, cultural level. The reality is that while coercive hierarchical power is still a dominant expression of leadership power (all over the world), power-based leadership is a culturally waning paradigm in all contexts, because we live in a wiki, prosumer culture. What I mean by that is that increasingly, people want to contribute to whatever they are a part of (including what they consume). And, increasingly, organizations of every stripe are decreasing hierarchies and moving toward flat organizational structures and the power of teams.

Sure, as I acknowledged in the introduction, we can argue semantics and reframe power in positive ways (like the power of servant leadership). But, for our purposes here, let's just stick with the more commonly understood (and exercised) concept of power: the ability and practice of exerting influence over others whether they want it or not. That's the kind of power I'd like to see (mostly) excised from church leadership. (I concede with a little "mostly" there, because if I were the executive pastor or senior pastor of a church today or if I were overseeing a number of paid staff in my current role, I'm sure there would be times when I would "exert influence over others when they didn't want it"—whether I'd be right or wrong is a separate conversation.)

A PARADIGMATIC SHIFT

Back in 2010, I read a wordy and exhausting book about teenagers that was, despite its weaknesses, full of diamonds (if one had the patience to look for them). That book was *Teen 2.0*, written by the former managing editor of *Psychology Today*, Dr. Robert Epstein.[7]

I had the very first cohort of my Youth Ministry Coaching Program read the book, and we had wonderfully lively conversations about some of those diamonds. I posted a review of the book on my blog, and the author commented! I took a little risk, and sent him a message at the email address he'd used with his blog comment. To my pleasant surprise, he responded quickly, and I discovered that he lived a short distance from my home.

I asked Epstein if there was any chance he'd be willing to meet with my cohort of youth workers to talk about his book, and he invited our whole group up to his home.

Somewhere in the midst of a freewheeling conversation about the infantilization and isolation of teenagers, Epstein's elementary-aged children arrived home from school and stomped through the house. I'd known that he had adult sons and realized this brood must be a second lap around the parenting track with a second marriage. I asked him: "With your current understanding of teenagers and how we tend to disempower them by treating them as children and isolating them, how has your parenting changed with this second set of children?"

Epstein didn't even blink. He responded: "I have tried to shift from parenting by control to parenting by facilitation." Then, after a short pause, he added, "And by facilitation, I mean identifying and nurturing competencies."

Bam.

Our little band of merry youth workers had some

amazing fodder for dialogue out of those two lines. We began by reflecting on and talking about our own approaches to parenting (for those of us who were parents). But we quickly shifted to a conversation about what the implications of this idea would be/could be for our youth ministries.

My wife and I had multiple conversations about these ideas and our own parenting—our two kids were in junior high and high school at that time. Jeannie and I were already committed to a counter-cultural approach to parenting teenagers that prioritized:

- Giving meaningful responsibility and expectation
- Providing a combination of support and freedom
- Not removing natural consequences to choices made

In short, we were already trying our hardest to not parent by control (the dominant approach to parenting these days, at least in middle-class and upper-middle-class contexts). And we regularly received overt and covert messages from other parents that we were not doing this thing right.

Epstein's words gave us a clearer agenda.

And I continued to have conversations with groups of youth workers about what it would look like to shift from control to facilitation in our approaches to youth ministry. Really, if we're fully honest, so much of what we do in youth ministry these days is about control:

- We try to control student behaviors.
- We try to control student beliefs.
- We try to control their media choices and language use and clothing preferences and so much more.

After a couple years of thinking about this idea of shifting from control to facilitation, it struck me that the same should be true for business and church leadership. And quickly on the heels of that realization, I had a moment of clarity: The notion of moving from a paradigm of control to a paradigm of facilitation resonates in parenting and youth ministry and business and church *because all of those are functions of leadership.*

Ultimately, this paradigmatic shift is a leadership principle, and it's very tied to the issue of power.

Let me state this clearly for our purposes in this

book: *Church leadership needs to move from a paradigm of control to one of facilitation.* In this context: *Facilitation means identifying and nurturing competencies.*

As I reflected on that leadership shift, I started to ruminate on different—let's call them "powerless"—approaches to leadership that would embody this shift. I developed nine metaphorical job titles to flesh out my ideas. I hope they'll stir your thinking and nudge you (and me) off balance a bit. I hope we can take them on a road trip together—test 'em out a bit. I'll unpack them one per chapter.

The invitation to you, as you read, is to look for two or three of the nine. I'd love you to identify one that you're already doing, even if you didn't have language for it previously (and I hope the relevant chapter provides you with that language). Then, I'd love you to notice *one or two more* that you connect with, resonate with. When you read these, you'll think, "That's totally how I'm wired, and in my wheelhouse, and I need to start living this out." I believe you have those leadership styles in you, ready to be mined and put into practice.

2
COMPETENCY FACILITATOR

When I was a 31-year-old junior high pastor at a large church in Pasadena, California, my senior pastor took me out for lunch on the anniversary of my hire. During lunch, he asked me what job I'd like to have someday in the future. I told him that I absolutely loved youth ministry and hoped to stay connected to it in one way or another for the rest of my life. But I also uttered an additional crazy thought: One day I'd love to be your executive pastor.

Apparently he heard me, because less than two years later that senior pastor asked me to take on the EP role. I was 33. I had bleached blonde hair and wore T-shirts and shorts to work. And this was a 100-year-old church with 20 pastors, well over 100 staff, and church attendance around 6000. The five associates who reported to me were all over 50 years old (including the 60-year-old former executive pastor, who'd been in that role for 20 years, but voluntarily "stepped down" to be the associate pastor of adult ministries).

Needless to say, it was a stretch. I heard through the grapevine that the church board thought the senior pastor was nuts (and maybe he was). One board member even told me, in a weird attempt to encourage me (I think), that he had incredulously asked, "Who in their right mind appoints the junior high pastor as the executive pastor?"

I have absolutely zero misunderstanding about this: I was under-qualified and under-experienced for this role. And I know I made plenty of mistakes.

But every time I sat down with the senior pastor to process stuff, he beamed at me with a genuine grin of excitement and belief. He constantly reminded me why he had chosen me for this role. He listed the skills and competencies he saw in me that were the right fit for this season. He gave me input and opinions when I asked for them but rarely told me what to do. And he robustly had my back when people came to him about decisions I'd made that they didn't like.

And: He gave me a metric ton of freedom to fail and

succeed and risk and lead change.

This senior pastor was my *Competency Facilitator*, identifying and nurturing potential he saw in me.

I admit this title is a little repetitive of the paradigmatic shift I just suggested. But *Competency Facilitator* is such a pregnant metaphor, such a potent imaginary job title.

As a *Competency Facilitator*, leadership leverages curiosity in noticing strengths, potentialities, and each person's unique made-in-God's-imageness. This leader is not exerting force on people but leading through nurturing. This leader's greatest contribution is to call out what others might not (yet) see in a person, or even what the person might not (yet) see about herself.

And, more than only calling out these competencies, this leader's role is to create supportive spaces for people to test-run these competencies. This leader supports, offers feedback, and continues to point out growth and development.

THIS IS NOT ABOUT MANAGEMENT

My definition of control is: *minimizing variables and maximizing efficiencies for predictable outcomes.*

In some ways, you might say that's the task of management. And management is not to be viewed as somehow inherently evil or bad. Of course not. But management is a very different mindset than that of the *Competency Facilitator*.

I mentioned Max De Pree's brilliantly-titled but otherwise just-okay book called *Leading Without Power* in the introduction. There's a story in this book that wonderfully shows the difference between a manager and, by inference, a *Competency Facilitator*:

> *Esther and I have eleven grandchildren. One of them born weeks premature is now in third grade, and while she has some special challenges, she is really doing quite well. One day when she was three years old, she came to visit me in my office, which is in a small condominium. She said, "Grandpa, would you like to see me run?" And I must tell you, my heart jumped. I thought to myself, this little girl can hardly walk. How is she going to run? But like a good grandparent, I said, "Yes, I'd like to see you run." She walked over to one side of the room and started to run, right across in front of my desk and directly into the side of a refrigerator. It knocked her on her back, and there she lay, spread-eagled on the floor with a big grin on her face. Like any good manager,*

I immediately went over with a solution. I said, "Honey, you've got to learn to stop." And she looked up at me with a big smile and said, "But, Grandpa, I'm learning to run."[8]

If you're a good manager, you're interested in problem solving and fixing what went wrong. But if you're a *Competency Facilitator*, you create space for people to run (and cheer them on when they do, even if they run straight into the side of a refrigerator).

A REAL-LIFE YOUTH MINISTRY EXAMPLE

I've been challenged in recent years about the importance of meaningful responsibility, particularly in terms of teenagers and young adults moving into adulthood. I witnessed a real-life example of this with my child Riley, when Riley was a junior in high school.

Riley was passionate about the earth's environment. To illustrate this, I should mention that almost every week, for about six months, Riley would walk about a mile to the closest Starbucks and ask to speak to the manager. Riley would then ask the manager why all Starbucks cups had a "Please Recycle" message on the bottom, but Starbucks (at that time) did not offer recycling bins. Of course, the managers of this Starbucks grew to expect the question, but it never stopped Riley from asking it week after week.[9]

Our church high school ministry had five small student leadership teams, and Riley was on two of them: the Praise team (Riley played keyboards and bass guitar in the youth worship band) and the Planet team (which collected recyclables from the church in order to provide funding for five sponsored children).

The model was that each of the five teams had an adult leader as the point person. For months, the high school pastor tried to find an adult to step into this role for the Planet team. But no one was interested or available. The team was struggling and at one point was almost defunct, with only Riley and one other member sorting through bags and bags of recyclables on a weekly basis. The whole thing was about to go under as they waited for a leader.

But one day our astute high school pastor switched out of a management mindset into a *Competency Facilitator* mindset and saw that Riley had all the passion and competency, even if a team without an adult leader wasn't the working model. He took a chance on Riley and asked Riley to lead the team.

Riley completely rose to the responsibility, recruiting a larger team, producing a recruitment video, training the team and hosting them for social stuff, and ensuring the work got done. It was a major win in terms of Riley's development and a great experience of owning meaningful responsibility.

MORE THAN NOTICING

That's a simple story, and it illustrates our need as leaders to break out of our mental maps as much as it illustrates this powerless leadership function.

But remember: A *Competency Facilitator* does more than notice competencies. That's a critical first step, of course. I really don't know if I'd be doing what I'm doing today if a youth pastor hadn't stopped me in the hallway at church when I was in seventh grade to tell me he thought I'd be a great youth pastor someday. That vision had a giant impact on me. But, honestly, that youth pastor didn't do anything to facilitate this vision—he merely named it.

This metaphorical job title is not Competency *Noticer* or Competency *Identifier*. The Facilitation aspect is critical—and the part that requires time, patience, and investment.

And of course, this role isn't just about competency in teenagers; this role applies to all our leadership relationships, not the least of which is with volunteers in church ministry.

So, who played the role of a *Competency Facilitator* in your life? And who in your world could use some competency noticing and facilitating?

3
CULTURE EVANGELIST

When it comes to organizational health, the internal culture makes all the difference in the world (this is true for youth ministries, for churches, for businesses, and every other sort of organization). A passionate, hopeful, even fun culture will lead to engagement, loyalty, trust, ownership, and productivity—even during difficult times. A lousy culture of suspicion, alienation, and dishonesty just makes everyone miserable, and all sorts of negative results become inevitable.

I spent a little over eleven years working at a ministry organization called Youth Specialties, which I mentioned in chapter one. It wasn't a huge staff at all— just 30–40 at any given time. And I saw a huge swing in our culture over those years.

For the first five or six years of my tenure, we were led by Mike Yaconelli, a passionate and generous wild man who cried as often as he laughed (which was often). He loved Jesus and loved giving gifts and had as much fun as a preteen with his remote-control fart machine. (Really.)

Those years were wonderful in many ways. And all of us loved working together, for the most part. But over time we developed some unhealthy patterns. Particularly, we at the leadership level developed a pattern of control. Outsiders wouldn't have seen it, but our staff felt it.

Mike died unexpectedly in a car accident in 2003, and we spent six months in corporate and personal shock, grieving the loss of our beloved leader. I was already the president at this time, but what it meant to be the president shifted dramatically overnight.

I don't take credit for the amazing years that followed immediately after that season. In most ways, I feel like I was just along for the ride. Karla, Mike's widow, often told our staff that Mike's death was his final gift to us, freeing us to step more fully into our future together. I'd been a part of some wonderful staff teams, but nothing came close to what we experienced in those three or four years.

We laughed more than we'd ever laughed. We cried together. We prayed together. We were honest. We collaborated. We were creative. We made tough decisions with confidence. And we grew like crazy, with more youth workers attending our events than ever before, and creating products and resources that were home runs.

It was the best organizational culture I've ever participated in. And then it wasn't.

Somewhere during those amazing years, a large Christian publisher bought us. They were good people who had partnered with us for years. And while there were massive headaches during the integration of backend stuff, they were intentionally hands off when it came to our culture. In fact, two CEOs in a row specifically told me that they knew not to mess with our culture, as it was the most important factor—other than any hard-to-measure blessing from God—contributing to our success. Sure, our staff Christmas parties got a little less wild and spendy. And spending in general got a few more guardrails. But overall, things were wonderful, even into the first year of the third parent-company CEO.

But then the economy took a sour turn in 2008. Churches stopped spending money, and we were rather quickly in deep trouble.

Now, an organization with a great culture (and some acumen in other areas) can survive deep trouble. But we lost sight of the importance of our culture, and it slipped through our fingers. Under massive pressure to "grow up" (those quotes are there for a reason), individually and organizationally, we moved into 18 months of some of the worst organizational culture I've ever been a part of. If I hadn't been in the #1 seat, I would have quit. And there are many times since then that I've wondered why I didn't leave, rather than slog through a year that likely took five years off my lifespan.

In the end, I lost my job—as did 85% of our team— and key parts of the organization were sold to another ministry.

I'm sure there are plenty of things I could have done differently. I'm so glad to be who I am today and where I am today; so, in a weird way, I am thankful for all that pain. But people were wounded and, paraphrasing the title of Chinua Achebe's famous work of African fiction, things fell apart.

No question, there were dozens of complex contributors, not the least of which were the economy and troubling interference from our corporate parent. But ultimately, the shift in our culture, I believe, is what did us in.

CULTURE CREATION

I'm becoming more and more convinced that one of the most important skill sets for a 21st-century leader is the ability to lead in the area of culture creation. In my book *Youth Ministry 3.0*, I wrote about the increased need for leaders (youth workers, in that case, but this is true for all church leaders) to move toward differentiated, contextually appropriate, discerned ministry values, structures, methods, and approaches.[10] For that to happen (particularly if we're moving away from top-down power structures), we have to re-learn the spiritual art of discernment. And we have to learn to practice discernment using a collaborative approach, as opposed to going off to a cave to get a "word from God."

One of the most important things we need to discern (remember: that means an active reliance on the Holy Spirit, not our own brilliance and insight) is culture. We need to collaboratively discern the current culture of our church (or youth group, or other ministry) and the culture we *aspire toward*.

The salient question becomes: *Who does God dream we*

could be?

Once this culture is understood, this powerless leader becomes an evangelist for that culture (hence: *Culture Evangelist*).

I'm not using the term "evangelist" here in the way Christians normally do. This is not about sharing the gospel of Jesus Christ. I'm using the term "evangelist" in the way that a company like Apple has in the past, giving people the word "evangelist" in their job titles. The job of the "iPad Evangelist," for example, was to spread the good news about iPads.

The job of the *Culture Evangelist* is to spread the good news about her organizational culture—what's currently beautiful about it and what's even more beautiful about where it's headed.

This is the one metaphorical job title in this book that was also someone's real job title. Through a friend, I met a passionate leader named Donavon—a former youth pastor—who was the "Lead Culture Evangelist" for Zappos Insights, the corporate training arm of Zappos.com (the massive online shoe retailer).[11] I loved Donavon's title. Church leaders need to unofficially adopt that title.

We evangelize: *This is who we are!*

We evangelize: *This is who we are called to become!*

We evangelize: *These are the things that are most important to us (our values)!*

At a gathering of junior high pastors several years ago, my friend Eric commented that in their youth ministry, they tried to embrace the idea that "the feel of the ministry is the most important content." Later, I heard Chap Clark, youth and family ministry guru and professor at Fuller Seminary, refine this to: "The method is the message."[12]

What does culture creation look like in your context?

How can you move toward it, then evangelize it?

4

MISSION CURATOR

My primary context is youth ministry, so allow me an archetypal story from that world.

Each year well over half of the paid youth workers in America experience a moment of stuckness at church budget-formation time. (Heck: This might be true in 90% of them, but I haven't done any real research on this other than observing hundreds of youth workers. So, I'm playing it safe and saying "over half.") The terminology might be different from church to church, but it usually looks something like this:

The youth worker sits at his or her desk, trying to come up with goals, not having any idea what to write down and knowing that there are likely some magic words and phrases that will appease. It's budget-creation time, and the youth worker is asked, along with coming up with a proposed budget, to develop a "ministry plan," which is simply church-y language for some goals that will justify the budget request and prove both the youth worker's loyalty to the church and his or her competence at delivering the good stuff.

The youth worker sits there, pondering. She thinks, "Ah, let's see... I know they're going to want to see numerical growth, so... *The youth ministry attendance will grow by 10%.* Ooh, yes, they *will* like that. But, where to go from there?" The youth worker knows that the *ministry plan* will never be looked at again once the budget is approved.

I used to have negative things to say about goal setting in organizations (including churches). But this was misguided and merely a reaction to the stupid way most churches address goals. Ministry leaders (those setting the goals) are basically throwing spaghetti at the wall to see what sticks, as they create goals in a complete vacuum, apropos of nothing.

Goals are important and critical to growth (any kind of growth). But they are *only* useful and helpful when they flow out of strategy, which flows out of values, which flows out of mission.

Here's that process in a forward direction:

Mission ("Why do we exist?")
↓
Values ("What are we called to embody in this season?")
↓
Strategy ("How will we embody the values?")
↓
Goals ("What action steps do we need to take and what measurements do we need in order to know if we're embodying the values?"

In other words: *why we exist* (leads to) *what we're passionate about* (leads to) *how we'll embody this* (leads to) *how we'll know if we're succeeding.*

WHAT IS MISSION?

We've all heard the importance of leaders articulating and embracing the mission of the organization. But I see four significant flaws in how this often plays out:

First, more often than not, church mission statements lean toward one-size-fits-all. If you look at 10 church websites and find their mission statement, you'll likely find that most of them could be applied to any church. When your church's mission statement isn't obviously reflecting the uniqueness of your church, something's wrong. The *something wrong* might be that the process of creating the mission statement was flawed. Or worse, it could be that your church doesn't actually know what its mission is.

Second, churches often create a mission statement merely to stick it on a website (and maybe on the bulletin)—a mission statement that sounds nice but doesn't actually shape how things are done. While creating a mission statement isn't necessarily bad, this surfacy approach misses the point. The mission of the organization (business, church, youth ministry) is difficult to fully capture in one or two carefully wordsmithed sentences. Those sentences are often cerebral, while the real mission is more gut. Real mission is the embodied fuel of why we exist. It's something that needs to be felt more than written into a sentence (I'm not suggesting that articulation is misguided, but mission is more than that).

Third, a leader creating a "mission statement" on her own often often develops it with an outdated (and unbiblical) hierarchical power mindset. A real mission is discerned. And, I would suggest, should be collaboratively discerned, not brought down from the mountain on stone tablets.

Finally, real mission (the kind that can be lived out) has an unrelenting core but liquid edges. Real mission has some fluidity. Real mission assumes a posture of humility and openness to change—not only in the implementation but in the mission itself. Real mission says, "This is who we believe God is calling us to be, for now; and we hope God will continue to reveal newness."

Mission provides rails for "where are we going?"

WHAT'S A CURATOR?

Curator is an important word choice here. A curator doesn't create everything. A curator creates space for interaction, participation, and enjoyment. A curator understands that her power is in the role of host, not dictator. A curator points to others, to works of beauty and discomfort, and never points to self. Really, a curator is a *user-experience engineer*.

You're probably most familiar with the title "curator" in the context of a museum. Imagine an art museum curator for a moment. Most large art museums have collections of art many times greater than the room on their gallery walls to display art. The curator's role starts with choosing which art will be displayed.

But the curator does more than that one task. The art museum curator is a user-experience engineer (or *experience designer*). They not only decide what art gets displayed but also...

- Put together (or invite in) special exhibits
- Consider the order of art in a particular gallery room
- Decide the exact location (think: height) of the art
- Choose lighting
- Decide what will, and what won't, get added to a little descriptive placard next to a piece of art and what summaries will be posted near a gallery or exhibit

All of this curation work is intended to help you and me, the museum visitors, engage with the art in specific ways, to increase our interest and understanding.

With that in mind, the *Mission Curator* is a powerless leader who passionately develops ways for people to interact with the organization's mission. Or, the *Mission Curator* leads by helping everyone bump into the focus of this church's reason for existence.

This engagement starts with insiders: staff and key stakeholders. But the engagement also extends to customers (in church world this would be church attendees) and those you're trying to reach. If outsiders connect with and resonate with the mission (not just the mission statement but tangible expressions of why we exist), they are substantially more likely to stick around.

MISSION DRIFT

Mission drift—the process of doing things that don't align with the mission—is an extremely dangerous road for organizations to go down and often results in decreased results, lowered morale, internal conflict, and an inability to know how to make the right decisions. Once mission drift begins (often with tiny increments), it becomes increasingly difficult to stop, much like a car drifting out of control. And of course, a car drifting out of control quite commonly results in a crash.

Let me provide three short examples from my own experience:

The small ministry organization I help lead—The Youth Cartel—started as only me, doing a variety of things to train and resource youth workers. In the earliest days, that included a lot of speaking engagements and writing projects, as well as the launch of our Youth Ministry

Coaching Program and an event, the Middle School Ministry Campference. But when my partner, Adam McLane, joined me, the Cartel suddenly felt like a real organization, and a multiplying effect took place.

We also greatly increased our overhead as we launched a publishing line and additional events, brought on some part-time contract workers, and initiated systems that cost money to have in place.

One of Adam's skill sets is all-things web related. He's brilliant at WordPress website design. And we started (really, he started) taking on a variety of consulting jobs that were actually website builds for others. Some of these were youth ministry organizations, which fit nicely into our mission:

> *The Youth Cartel's mission is to encourage and challenge adults who minister to youth through holistic professional coaching, strategic consulting, transformational events, and inventive resource development that advance youth ministry in new ways.*

But, as is often true when things are operating on a shoestring budget, we took on plenty of other web projects that were 100% outside of our mission. Honestly, we needed the money!

Eventually it became clear that this increasing amount of side-work, though financially helpful, was creating mission drift. Way too much of Adam's time—and more importantly, his creativity and energy—was being expended on projects that were off mission. It was a challenging financial decision to completely cut off this work, but it brought a renewed sense of commitment to our mission for both of us.

A second example:

Years ago, while I was at Youth Specialties, we launched into two new initiatives based on our competencies in publishing and running events. Seeing the rise of what was then referred to as the emerging church, we decided to come alongside this loose collection of revolutionary thinkers wrestling with new forms of church and partner with them on books and events. Concurrently, we gave in to the many requests from former youth workers who were now senior pastors and launched the National Pastors Convention.

In both cases, we were leveraging our organizational skills. And, in both cases, we were still serving the church (which is how we justified these choices). Both of these initiatives were, at least by their second years, very successful (I think we would have shut them down much more quickly if they hadn't been financially viable).

But for all their benefits, these programs were totally off mission for us. As much as we tried to justify them and wedge them into alignment with why we existed, they were a distraction from our mission. And we discovered—mostly in hindsight, but still while both events and the publishing line were performing well— that all of this was hurting us.

Full disclosure: These were pet projects (which often leads to mission drift). The emerging church stuff was my pet project, and the pastor's convention was Mike Yaconelli's pet project. Any attempt to claim they fit into our mission was absolute reverse engineering.

So, we gave them away. We gave the National Pastor's Convention to Zondervan publishing, who'd been a key partner on the event already, and we gave away the Emergent Convention to an organization called Emergent Village (also partners). The publishing line simply disbanded.

These were hard decisions but completely necessary to stop the drift.

One final example, from my church (where I am not on staff but have something of a front row seat, since

I'm close friends with the senior pastor and executive pastor and played a role in both of them coming to our church).

My church grew at an extremely fast rate in its early years. By the time I started attending in 1999, the church was something like a dozen years old and had grown to a weekly attendance of around 2000. In the close-to-two decades since then, we've only grown a tiny bit (to somewhere between 2300–2500). This slowdown, understandably, has raised some questions and caused a good deal of reflection.

The mission of my church was extremely clear in its early years, and everything (sometimes annoyingly so) was focused on reaching the unchurched. As our congregation grew and matured, it made sense that some of this focus would need to broaden. In many ways, I love my church—and its wide variety of ministries—more than ever. My perception is that they (we) have likely stepped into an era with a new or revised mission, even if that hasn't been articulated.

But then there's the rub of the growth stall. For a few years, we've made adjustments and started initiatives (that are very much in line with the mission); but growth has hovered at the same mark. This wouldn't be an issue for a church whose mission was a more churchy version of *We exist to take care of our own.* But my church has always been outreach oriented.

In recent years, conversations have begun to take place around the ideas of church-planting or multi-site development. The notion is: Maybe this current size is what God has for us, but we still want to reach more people and need a new tactic.

In the middle of these ruminations, we've had a couple opportunities to plant churches with existing pastors and an opportunity to fold a struggling church into ours as a "site." I haven't been at the table for most of these conversations, but I know we haven't moved on any of them. And I am so glad that we haven't. Here's why: Launching into one of these opportunities would be getting the cart before the horse. Or, to use the Mission/Values/Strategy/Goals flow I unpacked earlier in this chapter, launching one of these initiatives would be jumping to strategy and goals without a re-thinking of our mission and values.

My concern would be that jumping into one of these options (even though they are good options) would lead to mission drift. However, it might be that one of these options would be spot-on mission, if we take the time to first discern and re-define our mission and values.

THE IMPORTANCE OF MISSION CURATION

The *Mission Curator* is one of the most important powerless leadership roles in an organization. Helping insiders interact with and remember the mission has two massively important results:

- It brings passion, energy, and focus.
- It helps provide a central through-line for decision making and guards against mission drift.

I was going to write that the *Mission Curator* helps provide guardrails, but that's not quite the right metaphor. Instead, what comes to mind is Autopia. This classic Disneyland and Disneyworld ride (which has been replaced in more recent years by a Cars movie-themed ride) was an amazing experience for kids, because they actually got to steer the car and operate the accelerator and brakes. But there was a central rail down the middle of the track that prevented user-error from occurring (at least in side-to-side movement—it was still possible to get in trouble for ramming into the car in front of you).

This isn't about limiting expression or creativity. Of

course the *Mission Curator*, if truly operating without power, wouldn't be using authority or coercion to demand compliance to the mission anyhow. Instead, this leader helps people remember the center rail—what's true and beautiful about our mission. This leader reminds us of our calling and highlights stories that reveal that sweet spot.

The *Mission Curator* also helps us see how our current reality and ministry expressions aren't yet a full-enough embodiment of our mission.

A handful of years ago, at Willow Creek's Global Leadership Summit, Bill Hybels spoke, and I remember one profound truth from his talk. Hybels said something along these lines (I'm paraphrasing, from my memory of what he said):

> *We often talk of and understand leadership connected to vision—a leader is a person who sees where we need to go and points the way. But there's a small problem with that: Human organizations are made up of humans, and humans tend to like things the way they are. Humans have a tendency to resist change. Because of this, before a leader can hope to have people rally around 'where we're headed,' the leader must first help people understand why here isn't good enough.*

Before we point to there, we have to help people see the insufficiency of here. (author's paraphrase)

The powerless leader doesn't dictate this progression; the powerless leader curates the process, hosting the dialogue and discernment, showcasing beautiful examples of the mission as well as examples that bring discomfort and move us toward the mission or away from things that are off mission.

Oh, and while it's nice in somewhat hierarchical structures when the point person owns the role of *Mission Curator*, the role can effectively be carried out by someone else (or multiple people). However, if there's any hierarchy (which there normally is in 99.99% of organizations), it's absolutely critical that the #1 seat empower the *Mission Curator* or the role is almost impossible to carry out.

Start with this: Do you know what your church's mission is? Is it one-size-fits-all and useless? Or does it have "teeth"—providing encouragement, prodding, course correction, and new initiative discernment?

5
STORYTELLING HOST

*Let's start this meeting by having Claire share the
story of the interaction she had with a visitor last
week.*

*Instead of only sharing the numbers about our
recent youth group outreach event, I'd love to
read two stories I asked a couple of our volunteers
to write out.*

*Would it be possible to start including some very
short faith stories in our church newsletter? I'd be
happy to take point on collecting those.*

At the last church where I served as junior high pastor,
we developed a pattern at our monthly junior high
ministry volunteer meeting. We would gather on a

Sunday after church and eat together. Eating together, by the way, provides space for unforced conversations; and during unforced conversations, stories tend to be told, particularly when the conversation partners have a shared interest—in this case, junior high ministry.

After our meal, we would go over calendar items and other important communication bits. We usually had a short training segment of some sort. But then we always moved into my favorite section of our gatherings: Staff Person of the Month. I had purchased a box of used and damaged trophies from an engraving shop, super cheap (they had female swimmers on top!). And each month, I only had to pay for a little engraved plate that acknowledged the recipient.

During the preceding month, I intentionally watched for stories of our volunteers embodying one of our values. I chose a good story, and selected that person for the Staff Person of the Month (they also got a nifty little certificate, in addition to the trophy!), and had them tell that story. I usually framed that time by reminding everyone of the value and then opened up the floor for others to share stories that revealed or connected with that value.

STORIES THAT EMBODY VALUES

Stories are wonderful for myriad reasons. But the *Storytelling Host* is particularly interested in identifying and giving platform to stories that embody the ministry's values. So, let's take a moment and talk about values.

I'm convinced that leading from values is one of the most identifiable factors in differentiating great leadership from good leadership (or bad leadership). Values flow out of mission but are more seasonal in nature (as in, this chapter of our ministry life together). Remember: Values are the answer to the question "What are we called to embody in this season?"

These days, I notice that many churches have a set of values listed on their websites (and, I assume, listed elsewhere). But, much like mission statements, I hardly ever see a list of values that have much usefulness. Most of them fall into one (or both) of two uselessness buckets:

- One-word and short-phrase values are surprisingly unhelpful. If I told you that my church's values are Discipleship, Community, and Worship, that would tell you *very little* about my church. And because values expressed in this modality are always open to interpretation, needing further unpacking and explanation, they are decidedly impractical for creating strategy, or for any sort of decision-making or evaluation.

- Values that express a general ecclesiology (what every church should be about) don't provide teeth for the chomping action of strategy, goals, plans, and evaluation. I regularly tell my coaching cohort participants, as they're developing values, that their values need to have teeth, or "be more toothy." A church's (or individual ministry's) values should be wonderfully unique. If I knew something about three churches and had their values in front of me without church names attached, I should be able to quickly identify which set of values belongs to which church.

This *leading from values* stuff is so indispenably critical that I've considered, multiple times, adding *Values Clarifier* or *Values Shepherd* as a tenth metaphorical job title in this list. But ultimately, I haven't done this for two reasons: First, values need to be embedded in and reflected by every one of these nine means of leading without power. And second, the process of collaboratively discerning values really does need to be initiated by and shepherded by the person in charge (even if they bring in help). If the ministry's point person (or point people) aren't in alignment with the discerned values, the values either won't get used or tensions will arise.

But I want to unpack the process I've developed for collaboratively discerning values, and this is as good a place as any, since the *Storytelling Host* role is ridiculous without great values to tell great stories about.

COLLABORATIVELY DISCERNING VALUES

I sort of stumbled onto the process of developing good organizational values. And it was in the context of some horrible leadership on my part—the sort of manipulative, coercive use of power this book stands against.

Earlier, I mentioned the difficult time our staff at Youth Specialties went through after the untimely death of our founder and friend, Mike Yaconelli. After about six months of grieving, a few of our most forward-thinking staff came to me. They told me, "We understand why this time of pausing was needed. But it's quickly starting to feel like we're stuck. And we're desperately in need of change. We don't mean this as a threat, but if things don't start to change, we don't think we'll stay much longer."

Okay, then! Time to jump-start some change! My stupid thinking was: What we really need right now are some new creative products—new books, new events, new marketing programs.

I had just read marketing guru Seth Godin's book, *Purple Cow*, a book about the importance of truly unique products and marketing.[13] I handpicked 15 of our 30 staff, choosing those I perceived as the most creative and the least change-resistant. I bought them all a copy of *Purple Cow*, asked them to read it, and took them on a three-day "Purple Cow Retreat" to a large rented house in Palm Springs, California. I realize this was a risky proposition, especially since half of our staff weren't invited. But I felt like we needed something akin to defibrillation on our organizational heart.

Excitement was high as we settled into our quirky and large Old School Palm Springs digs. These people were salivating for change and eager to get to it. I had decided to start with a little exercise to get us primed up and all on the same page. Problem was: It was 100% manipulative.

I stood at a flip chart with a big marker and said, "Okay,

this is great! Before we get going on thinking up some great new stuff, I thought it would be good to stack hands on some of our values."

Yes, I used the word *values*, but I didn't know what I was talking about. I just wanted people to name what was awesome about us, so we could have a warm, fuzzy, super-feel-good starting point.

I wrote the word VALUES across the top of the page and made my first bullet point, waiting for the first upbeat and encouraging statement. But none came.

Everyone was silent.

I rephrased: "You know, like, what are those things that we all agree on and that are awesome about us? What do we really like about working here?"

Crickets.

I started to panic and offered a for-instance, filling in the space by that first bullet point, saying: "Like, you know, we all love that this is such a fun place to work!" (I wrote: *We value fun!*)

More crickets, now accompanied by folded arms and faces revealing a commitment to resistance. They were, every one of them, silently-but-loudly proclaiming to me: *We will not be pawns in your game.*

After a long and tortuous silence, one of our vice presidents raised his hand. If you're leading a brainstorming session and someone raises his hand, asking permission to speak, you know you're in trouble. I pointed at him, and he sighed loudly, then asked, "Do you just want us to give you the answers you're looking for, or can we be honest?"

Everything in me wanted to plead, "Just give me the answers I'm looking for!" But I was completely cornered and really had no option but to say, "Of course, I'd love you to be honest."

They all knew I was lying (the sweat on my forehead was probably a good indication), but they chose to trust the moment anyhow. Another person spoke up—my best friend on staff—and said, "Well, I know we like to think we offer freedom to our employees, but we really value control."

When leading a brainstorming session, one of the rules, of course, is that everything gets written on the board. That's why I found myself writing "We value control with our employees" next to the second bullet point.

74

I have to credit those courageous staff, because they really did get honest, in the presence of those who had the power to fire them or sideline them. The floodgates opened, and in about 30 minutes we filled up about five of those giant sticky-pad pages with a massive bulleted list of what I've come to call Current Values.

Funny thing: Mixed in with the tough truths were all the good things I'd hoped to cajole out of them in the first place. But the list was more comprehensive and truthful. It was an exhaustive brain-dump of everything we currently valued. And by the end, even I could tell we were onto something.

Fast-forwarding: We worked through the process I'll describe below, finding our way by intuition, and ended up with a list of values—some existing and some aspirational—that provided us a basis for a bunch of strategic decision-making. And all of that led to some of our best years as an organization.

In The Youth Cartel's coaching program, we encourage youth workers to develop three sets of values, and we lead them in the process of two of those sets. The three we encourage are Ministry Values, Personal or Family Values, and what we call Personal Vocational Values (values that must be present for me to thrive in my work and for my church to receive my best contribution). Developing Personal Vocational Values is a solo endeavor. But Ministry Values are, we believe, best developed through a process of collaborative discernment.

After all, your best and most brilliant attempts at brainstorming will never be as amazing as tapping into God's dreams for your church or ministry.

Step one is to create a Values Discernment Team.

I suggest that this should not automatically be any pre-existing group (the church board, the whole youth ministry volunteer team, the church staff). This group should be off-book, not announced or put on a public calendar or opened up for whoever would like to participate. In fact, selecting the right people for this team is just about the most important step.

Some guidelines for asking the right people:

- They need to have spiritual maturity and an active prayer life.
- They need to be supportive of the ministry but not have a personal agenda.
- Some diversity is good, but it's not a democracy.

The best values discernment teams have 4–8 on them (less or more makes the process increasingly difficult, either diluted or encumbered or forced).

Here's the four-meeting process we teach in our coaching program. These can be effectively done in a 24-hour offsite retreat or over a series of weeks. At each meeting, remind the participants that this is a discernment process not a brainstorming session and that the whole thing should be an act of prayer.

Oh, and a little pro tip: Use one of those large Post-It flip charts for all this work, so every bit of the process can remain in view as you work through the meetings.

Meeting 1: Make a massive list of everything your ministry currently values: good, bad, and ugly.

In-between: Have someone record the list in a document and distribute it to the group. Ask participants to prayerfully consider which of these items is good and beautiful and needs to be protected.

Meeting 2: Identify the 2–4 items on that list that are the most beautiful and central to the mission and desired culture of the ministry, and write them as "existing" or "old" values that must be protected.

In-between: Ask participants to return their attention to the original list of current values, and prayerfully consider which are the most destructive to who they believe God is calling us to be.

Meeting 3: Identify the 2–6 worst offenders of current values that are destructive to the culture you want to create in your group, then write an inverse statement, and list them as "aspirational" or "new" values.

In between: Distribute the short lists of Old/Existing Values and New/Aspirational Values. Ask participants to prayerfully consider if there's something missing, something new.

Meeting 4: Wordsmith the values you've identified, then consider if anything is missing, something new.

Your end goal is to come up with 5–8 values, written as complete sentences. I actually encourage ministries to include a value sentence and one or two sentences of clarification.

Here are a couple actual samples from one of the youth workers who went through the Youth Ministry Coaching Program and led this process with a team from his church:

- **Jesus calls us into ministry with the poor.**
  We want our ministry to be clearly in alignment
  with God's heart for justice. In this way, we
  value solidarity with the poor, not just
  acts of charity. Loving others is essential
  to being a disciple of Jesus.

- **Studying Scripture is how we grow in our
  faith.** Learning God's story and how we
  fit into the story helps us to learn more about
  God and our place in the world.

Once the values are complete, they should become a
tool for active use. They should be a decision-making
grid. They should be an evaluative tool. And they
should even be the dominant metric for measuring
success (and lack of success).

BACK TO THE STORYTELLING HOST

Once the values are in place, a key role of the powerless
leader is to host storytelling.

Because: Storytelling is one of the primary means
of culture creation. If we hope to see our ministries
embody and live out values, telling stories that reflect
those values is critical. Merely printing the values
and taping them on the wall has little impact. But we

humans—and even more so, we Jesus-followers—are moved by story. Particularly in a postmodern culture, we understand ourselves, our affinities, our personal values, and our resonance with the values of the organization, through story. Story is the vehicle for truth (and this is not new—certainly, this was the experience of all the original audiences of the Bible, Old Testament and New).

The word "host" is critical here. The powerless leader doesn't merely tell stories constantly (though telling stories is good, and it would be difficult to be a good *Storytelling Host* without knowing how to effectively tell a story); leading without power means that we act as a host, creating spaces and environments where values-laden stories are told, where key moments in our history are re-told, where imaginative stories about our future are dreamed.

The *Storytelling Host* understands that her role is played out in two functions: story collection and story dissemination.

I was struck by these truths a few years back when I spent two days at Zappos.com, the online shoe retailer known for their internal culture as much as their business success. Particular stories from the history of the organization were told again and again, with great pride, from various staff (for instance, the story of the longest customer service call—more than eight hours—was seen as a great badge of honor, something everyone in the organization was proud of).

One of the ways any ministry leader can play this out is by making sure a regular part of a team meeting is storytelling. Stories of wonderful conversations and small group times, stories of glorious failures, stories of who we are and why our ministry exists, stories of mission, stories of values, stories of vision, and even stories of goals.

How are you, as a leader, hosting storytelling? How can you ramp this up—not just by becoming more of a storyteller yourself, but also by hosting an environment of storytelling?

6

CHAMPION OF HOPE

I've been doing more than my normal share of thinking about hope over the last several years. In some ways, it all started when I was asked to speak on the subject of hope at a youth ministry event very early in 2010. But the week after that talk on hope, I found myself in Haiti, just three weeks after the devastating earthquake that left the country in ruins and more than 100,000 people dead.

I had a profound, life-changing experience standing in the middle of a crowded street. I'd thought I was standing in the middle of a protest, but got confused when two grinning old women grabbed my hands and indicated that I was supposed to start dancing with them. Suddenly, I realized that this crowd wasn't protesting but were singing a praise song. All of them were beaming with joy.

In that awkward and disorienting moment, a verse
I'd memorized as a child popped into my head,
Romans 5:3-5: "We also glory in our sufferings,
because we know that suffering produces perseverance;
perseverance, character; and character, hope. And hope
does not put us to shame, because God's love has been
poured out into our hearts through the Holy Spirit, who
has been given to us."

I was then smacked upside the head with this thought:
These people are experiencing a level of hope that I
have never experienced, and it's expressly *because of*
their suffering.

We Americans have swallowed a lie, that optimism and
hope are the same thing. Hope merely becomes wishful
thinking. I'm a big fan of optimism, by the way; I just
no longer believe it's the same thing as hope.

In my book *Hopecasting*, which grew out of the
disequilibriating experience of the last few paragraphs,
I define hope as *a confident assurance that God
continues to author a story that leads us from belief to
action.*[14]

ORGANIZATIONAL HOPE

One of the tiny gifts I found in Max De Pree's book, *Leading Without Power*, (other than the title) that got me thinking about all of this many years ago, was a chapter on the function of hope, where De Pree discusses what I would call Organizational Hope.[15] In it, De Pree suggests that it's not only individuals who do or don't have hope—organizations either embrace hope or are mostly devoid of hope.

While this isn't talked about often, it's intuitively true. We've all been part of, or visited, organizations (churches, businesses, whatever) that lack hope and ones that seem to be bursting with hope. I can categorically tell you (and I'm sure you've seen this also) that it is quickly obvious if a church has hope or not.

Really, this isn't just Christian organizations—my visit to Zappos.com, the online shoe retailer, gave me a visceral experience of hope embodied, which I'll share in a bit.

But the leader who wants to lead without power (because, really, there's no way to hierarchically force someone to have hope!) becomes a *Champion of Hope* in the organization. The powerless leader listens for and is present to suffering—

not brushing past it or sweeping it under the rug. (Easier said than done, by the way. Particularly if you, as a leader, are a partial cause of that suffering). And in the midst of that safe articulation of struggle, the powerless leader points people to the source of hope (Jesus), rather than cul-de-sacs of optimism, technique, and other hope thieves.

The *Champion of Hope* provides reminders of who we place our hope in; reminders of what our hope feels like; reminders of why we have hope. They cultivate a language of hope and champion the belief that God is still authoring a story.

A CASE STUDY

In the midst of my initial framing of the ideas in this book, I had the wonderful opportunity to travel to Las Vegas and visit Zappos.com. I spent two days at the Zappos Insights Bootcamp, learning with 25 other business leaders from around the world how Zappos runs a very profitable business passionately anchored in 10 core values, with a vision of "delivering happiness."

What I saw was that the leadership of Zappos totally embodies this, even while they may not necessarily know the ultimate source of hope or even use language about hope. On one hand, I find this beautiful and amazing, that the grace of God allows hope to so permeate an organization that doesn't exist for the Kingdom; but on the other hand, this makes me a bit melancholy, realizing how few churches reflect the same.

Here's a journal entry I wrote at that time:

> *Delivering Happiness. Zappos is all about delivering happiness, to employees, vendors, customers.*
>
> *I sensed some internal resistance to this idea during the two days of Bootcamp. I wondered if—from my Christian mindset—joy would be a better framework than happiness. Happiness is, I reasoned, a nice-but-temporal feeling, tied to circumstances, whereas joy is deeper and more internal. But during the second day, I decided I was just being arrogant and condescending, imposing my own self-righteousness on a thing of true beauty.*
>
> *The Zappos employees do seem happy. And the handful of customers I've interacted with, either during my visit or in my own conversations, sure seem to be happy about Zappos.*

Maybe that's enough for a for-profit business like Zappos. It's certainly more than any other business delivers!

But it has continued to nag at me.

Two weeks later, I wrote this entry:

Happiness is awesome, a very wonderful and noble thing to deliver. It doesn't need to be discarded for something else; but just as the vision of Zappos has "evolved" from "largest selection" to "best customer service" to "delivering happiness," I think there might be a natural next step, an evolution, something transcendent:

Hope.

What if Zappos can deliver hope?

What if that's what they're already doing?

Certainly, during my 65 minutes of eavesdropping while a customer service agent named Pat spoke with a lonely costumer from Appalachia, she delivered something more than happiness. Yes, she delivered happiness, but there was something spiritual, something transcendent about what Pat

provided to this lonely man. She gave him hope.
Her patient listening, validation, and treating
him with dignity—treating him as a person worth
spending an hour with—had to offer him an in-
ternal, and not merely external or circumstantial,
sense of goodness in the world.

Pat offered possibility and potential. And I'm
quite confident that the hope that man experienced
had some kind of refining, transforming, yes, even
transcendent aspect to it. I think that man and
his whole existence was—in some immeasurable
way—changed. I think the trajectory of his life
was, in a way that could only be measured in the
tiniest of fractions, altered. But this fractional
shift in trajectory could have significant long-term
impact.

Some would quickly dismiss this as hyperbole and
suggest that it's absurd to say that an online shoe
retailer could offer something transcendent like
hope. But what if it's not an exaggeration? What
if Zappos (and other companies, for that matter)
could provide a sense that, out of our dissatisfac-
tion with the way things are, something better is
possible.

Hope isn't wishful thinking or optimism: Hope is

longing wrapped in expectancy.

My fellow Christians might not think this is possible apart from faith. But if we (Christians) consider real hope to be much more than wishful thinking or optimism, how can we not apply that definition to the experience of the lonely man on the hour-long call, even if he is completely unaware of the hope he's experiencing; even if Pat is only nominally aware of the hope she has dispensed?

I think it's likely that every church, every ministry, has Champions of Hope in their midst. They are often Champions-of-Hope-in-Waiting, because they haven't been given permission, they haven't been invited to lead the charge.

Maybe being a *Champion of Hope* isn't totally in your wheelhouse. But maybe you have the influence to notice a *Champion of Hope* and set them loose, set them free.

7

UNIQUENESS DJ

Most of us have been to wedding receptions where the DJ is nothing more than a weird dude with a "popular reception songs" playlist on a laptop. He hits play, takes a few requests, and hosts a few sometimes-creepy elements of the reception. I don't think I'll forget when the DJ at my lovely and pure niece's reception emceed the bit where the groom removes a garter from the bride's leg, then tosses it to all the single guys in an extremely odd macho push for a loop of satin and lace. This DJ kept shouting to the groom, as the groom removed the garter from my niece's leg, "Reach higher! Higher! Come on, higher!" It was tacky and would have made real DJs want to punch that guy in the throat. (Come to think of it, my brother-in-law, the bride's father, just about did punch him in the throat.)

This is *not* the image of a DJ I'm suggesting here. (We shouldn't use the term DJ for those guys. They should just be called Playlistmen.)

Instead, real DJing is an art that rose up first in the poorer boroughs of New York during the disco era. Traditional DJ equipment includes two turntables (for vinyl records), a switching mixer that determines if the music coming through the speakers is from one turntable or the other or both, and a set of headphones so the DJ can listen to tracks without the audience hearing (today there are all sorts of digital versions of this original set-up).

The DJ speeds up or slows down one of the turntables in order to "beatmatch" a track with what's playing on the other turntable. This allows for nonstop music with no breaks or pauses. DJs often play small riffs off a song track, repeating it while mixing in other music on top or providing a musical base on which a rapper can perform. DJs even get inventive by introducing alternate sounds, moving a record quickly back-and-forth to create "scratching," and other inventions.

This is the DJ metaphor I want you to hold in your mind.

THE DISPARATE JUNIOR HIGH MINISTRY TEAM AT MY CHURCH

The team of junior high ministry volunteers at my church is, I think, pretty amazing. And it's pretty odd, too. There are about a dozen young- to mid-twentysomethings. Most of them are in college and working part-time jobs. For the most part, they have a good amount of flexibility and availability, tons of energy, a willingness to try things and take risks, all mixed in with the normal turmoil and upheaval of young adult life.

We have a new couple who just joined us: no-kids-yet late-twentysomethings, into the first stages of their professional lives and married life.

Our junior high pastor is 30, married, and has a little kid.

Then there's John, Steve, and me. We're all over 50 years old. John is the oldest, at about 60. He's a retired middle school vice principal with adult children out on their own, who now manages some apartments. Steve is a 50-year-old mortgage broker with one son, a high schooler. And I'm a 53-year-old ministry leader with two college-aged kids.

Honestly, this team, taken collectively, has very little in common other than our love for Jesus and the fact that we like junior highers.

The leader of this ministry has a couple options:

The most common approach would be to squish each of us into a uniform mold: This is what a junior high ministry volunteer at our church does. This fits right in, naturally, with our previous description of control: *minimizing variables* and *maximizing efficiencies for predictable results*. And this approach *might* produce mostly predictable results (come on, we're talking about junior high ministry here!); but I promise you, the results will not be as good as they could be. Predictable? Somewhat. Uniform? Mostly. But tasty, rich, and complex? Not a chance.

Control might make a nice vanilla, but you need a different approach if you're hoping for Rocky Road.

THE UNIQUENESS DJ STEPS UP TO THE TURNTABLES

Our first powerless leadership metaphor, in chapter two, was *Competency Facilitator*. That metaphor plays out mostly at an individual level—identifying and facilitating competencies in individual people (particularly in other leaders, I would suggest).

The *Uniqueness DJ* role works in partnership with that skill to mix a team's uniquenesses into a cohesive whole. She is intentional about bringing together disparate people into something new and refreshing, honoring the components while envisioning something that's greater than the sum of the parts.

The *Uniqueness DJ* is not into pigeonholing people based on predetermined roles.

The *Uniqueness DJ* does not leverage traditional hierarchical power to assign people.

The *Uniqueness DJ* abhors vanilla and loves to create new mixes of surprisingly complementary flavors.

Wearing this hat (probably a cool porkpie, by the way), this leader allows for—celebrates, even—the one-of-a-kind gifting, experience, and personality of each person on the team and looks for ways to connect them to the shared values.

Here's a practical example: For years, in youth ministry, I utilized a highly articulated "job description" for volunteers. The thinking was (I had been taught this and subsequently taught this myself in many seminars) that youth ministry volunteers would flourish if they knew what was expected. I read that sentence now, and I think, *what a dehumanizing approach to people*.

I would approach this very differently today. After the shared values of the ministry are discerned and articulated, I would work with each volunteer—based on his or her strengths, interests, experiences, and competencies—to help him or her develop a unique plan for embodying our values in the context of their youth ministry calling. And, I would be intentional about how these unique works of art, made in the image of God, can experience something greater than themselves by bringing their uniqueness to the whole.

This kind of "mixing" isn't a blender approach, creating a mushy paste of liquefied banality. Instead, it's a skill more akin to a Ben and Jerry's flavor creator. Or, a super-fresh mash-up of disparate musical pieces overlaid on the beats of shared values.

Now let's hear some beats and scratching.

8
CONTEXTUALIZATION CZAR

Meredith is a youth worker and was in one of my North Carolina cohorts of the Youth Ministry Coaching Program. And she's a freaking rock star.

Meredith had been a youth intern at a large church, then left to attend seminary. While in seminary, she was involved in some sort of ministry effort that involved multiple small churches. And in that context, a vision was birthed. When Meredith's freshly minted husband (also a minister, but of the "One in Charge" variety) got placed in a small church in far-Western North Carolina, Meredith started to dream and scheme, plan, and pray. She knew the Methodist churches in Appalachia were all tiny and that few—if any—could support a youth ministry.

Meredith and four local pastors (including her husband) put together a grant proposal and got funding for a few years of startup. She met with ten small churches in her district and shared a vision for a *shared* youth ministry. All ten jumped in. And they were off, creating a beautiful ministry expression that is unique and quirky and powerful.

Check out these realities that are so contextualized and amazing:

The 10 churches have something like five pastors between them (more than one of the pastors have a "multi-point charge," meaning they preach at multiple churches).

- Most of these churches have between six and 50 people in them.
- Five of the churches do not even have a single child or teenager, yet they're on board and fully supportive (and involved).
- The youth group meetings rotate to a different church occasionally.
- Meredith has about 15 teenagers coming regularly—and get this: She had so many adults (mostly parents) showing up to help (too many for the youth ministry), she started an adult

small group that meets concurrently with the overflow of parents.

Meredith's context is certainly unique. And what's next, when the grant runs out, is still unclear.[16] But Meredith has developed a deep love for—and localized understanding of—the "mountain people" (as she calls the people in her community).

I'm deeply convinced that the very best youth ministries will always be highly contextualized and borne out of discernment from the Spirit's leading. Meredith and her one-of-a-kind youth ministry are embodiments of those two realities.

A FUNNY THING HAPPENED TO YOUTH CULTURE

For decades, youth culture was something of a monolith. Sure, there were all sorts of cliques and classifications and variants within youth culture. But the average American high school was a pyramid of social influence. This is why Young Life, the wonderful parachurch youth ministry organization that pioneered taking the gospel to teenagers on their own turf, used to tell campus workers, "Reach the key influencers, and you can reach the whole school." In most locations, the inference was, if you can reach the football team captain and the cheerleading team captain, their social influence would move through the whole school eventually. It was a sort of Reaganomics trickle-down approach to teenage social systems.

But sometime around the turn of the millennium, there was a massive shift in youth culture. Some would say this was due to the rise of the Internet, but my belief is that the Internet was merely rocket fuel on the change that was already taking place.

The shift, I believe, took place because my generation, Baby Boomers, are the first generation of Americans who looked backward, trying to hold on to their youth, rather than looking forward to what used to be the *benefits* of old age (rest, a caring family around you). In looking backward, we Baby Boomers elevated youth culture, which had previously been a subculture. We made it the dominant culture in America, and we continue to worship at the altar of youth (which, I'll admit, is a bit paradoxically odd, since we isolate and diminish youth so extensively).

Well, youth culture wasn't going to have any of this. Because one of the core tasks of being an adolescent is autonomy—wrestling with how I'm unique and how my choices make a difference—youth culture preferred to be *other* rather than *dominant*. Youth Culture responded by splintering and going underground. The dominant youth culture (pop culture) we all see is not the real-world space in which teenagers live. It's only the place they surface to interact with us old timers.

Today, instead of one monolithic youth culture, there are hundreds, even thousands, of youth cultures. The football team captain has very little influence on the whole high school. He might have influence on a small circle of other football players and assorted jocks and hangers-on who share his outlook and values. But the majority of teenagers in that high school could give a rip what he thinks, and he has no influence on them.

This has massive implications for youth ministry. For starters, every youth ministry is multicultural, whether it has racial or economic diversity or not.

But this shift, in addition to dramatically elevating a need for belonging, has led to tribalism. And in a culture marked by tribalism, context is everything.

Increasingly, our broader culture (where adults live) is marked by tribalism also, with diversity prized over conformity and individualism far surpassing institutional allegiance. Of course, this shift has been difficult for traditional institutions, including denominations that have long relied on institutional loyalty for attendance, membership, and giving.

But here's the germane implication for this chapter: While copying ministry approaches from other churches may have worked to some extent in the 1980s, it doesn't work anymore (and I think I could make a case for why it was never the best option).

APPOINTING A CZAR

We are all familiar with the title *czar*, at least from a miniscule grasp of Russian history. But that title took on new meaning when US presidents started appointing czars as executive branch subject leaders. As I write this, the US government has 38 people with *czar* in their title, ranging from "AIDS czar" to "Asian carp czar," and from "copyright czar" to "Gulf claims compensation czar."

In this context, a czar acts as a *subject matter expert* and *communication roundhouse* for various branches and programs of government. If the Fish and Wildlife Service, for example, needs to share or gain information or work collaboratively with the Environmental Protection Agency and the Department of the Interior about the problem of invasive Asian carp, the Asian carp czar is *the man* (or *the woman*, as I have absolutely no idea who the Asian carp czar currently is).

That's the metaphorical title we're using here: a subject matter expert, a clearing house of information, a connecting point or docking station for various ministries and programs who need to work together.

Now, let's apply that to the world of tribes and splintered culture.

CONTEXTUALIZATION CZAR AS ANTHROPOLOGIST

In order to actively engage in most of the previous metaphors, and in order to lead via collaboration, the leader who aspires to lead without traditional hierarchical power has to become an intentional student of context. Really, since we're living in an era where culture has splintered (youth culture, for sure, but all culture is following), the role of the leader must shift.

In the 1950s (think *Mad Men* or the church version of it—even more power but slightly less cigarettes and grain alcohol), the primary approach to leadership called for the loudest voice, and maybe the ability to think forwardly.

In the 80s and 90s, all kinds of social science-like skills rose up the "skills leaders must possess" ladder: empathic listener, prophetic visionary voice, new idea

103

generator, motivational speaker, and strategy hound.

But today, in our new world—when copying the other guy (or the other business, or the other church) gets you nowhere other than a few steps behind or grossly misguided—the ability to host these collaborative questions trumps the other "skills":

- What's our context?
- Who are we called to be?
- What are we passionate about, and why?
- What's unique to us?
- How can we become more us, rather than more like someone else?

This means that we have to be anthropologists. Wikipedia says, "Anthropology asks 'what defines homo sapiens?'"[17] Do you see the connection? It's pretty easy to translate that for our local, rather than global, realities. "What defines us here at The Youth Cartel?" Or "What defines us at First Church?"

Now, leaders have played this role in many ways over the decades and millennia. But the spirit of what we're addressing in this book is that power-based leadership is both unbiblical and ineffective in today's world. So, we have to think about how to ask the "what defines us" question without forcing or demanding or unilaterally deciding.

The *Contextualization Czar* is passionate about researching and learning about context, which includes:

- What is unique about our region?
- What is unique about our city or town?
- What is unique about our neighborhood?
- What are this church or ministry's theological convictions and tension points?
- What's the history of this church or ministry?
- What pain points in our history have defined us or continue to shape us?
- What successes in our history have defined us or continue to shape us?
- Who are the people God has already placed in our midst, and what are the things they care about?
- Who are the people God is compelling us to reach, and what are the things they care about?

And, of course, many more questions about context.

A friend of mine was one of the pastors at my church, but decided he had a specific calling to plant a church in a neighboring suburb that hit the contextual sweet spot for that community. My church is more of a regional church, with attendees coming from all over the San Diego area (and from all walks of life). But this friend once said to me: "I want to plant a church for guys with gun racks in their pick-up trucks, with two kids and a faithful dog, who watch football and drink beer." He knew his context (which, by the way, was the community he'd grown up in), and today his church is flourishing. Its parking lot is full of pick-up trucks with gun racks, and the seats are full of football-watching, beer-drinking, dog-owning middle-aged dads (and their families).

I've taken to telling youth workers this observed truth: *Everywhere* I go in the world (not only in the US), the best youth ministries are always weird. They have a high level of self-awareness about their uniquenesses and are proud of them. They celebrate their uniqueness and allow it to become part of their shared culture.

This isn't only true for youth ministries, of course. The same is increasingly true for churches and other ministries.

And that brings us back to… collaborative discernment.

Because: Discovering context is one thing, but knowing how to respond to it is another. The *Contextualization Czar* in not merely a data collector; this leader helps the rest of us create ministries and programs and systems that make sense in our context.

I believe the primary skill set needed (but not present) in most church leadership today is recovering the art of spiritual discernment. Understanding context, being responsive to context, and hosting collaborative discernment rooted in context might be the best gift you can give your organization.

9
TRUST GUARD

In one ministry I led, there were two times when we had to make the difficult decision to lay off a number of staff. In the first of those instances, the remaining staff trusted me, and in the second instance, they did not.

The first time was a painful-but-needed re-organization, a strategic decision flowing out of and deeply connected to a clarification of some aspirational values. It was absolutely the right decision, but that didn't make it any easier. I cared about every one of the six employees we were releasing, and some of them were close friends of mine. Maybe there was a chance that their lives and vocations would move to an even better place over time; but I know the pain, anxiety, and demeaning feelings of being let go—and I hated being the instigator of those realities.

The day after the lay-offs, our remaining staff gathered. I tried to share an explanation of the decision our leadership team had made. But in the middle of talking, I got choked up and momentarily couldn't continue. I stood in front of our staff, silent, with tears in my eyes and the occasional gulp of air. It was not fabricated at all (in fact, I tried my hardest to suppress this emotional and physical response!). My mind was racing, and I was concerned that this emotion might reveal an uncertainty about what we'd just done.

But it had just the opposite effect. My vulnerability (and subsequent honesty about why I was experiencing these strong emotions) shaped an environment of trust. While no one was excited about the lay-offs, our team rallied together and moved with additional boldness into a new reality.

The second round of lay-offs, six years later, was a totally different experience. I had been instructed by my boss (the CEO of our parent company) that if I hoped to avoid having our organization sold off or shut down, I needed to prove that we were willing to take drastic steps, including cutting millions of dollars out of our budget. This CEO guessed that this would mean laying off about half of our staff.

Sure enough, when my leadership team and I crunched

the numbers, the only way to cut as deeply as expected was to lay off 15 of our 30 staff. How we would survive this cut was somewhat unclear, though we were certainly going to try. I felt stuck between a rock and a hard place. I wasn't in agreement with this choice, but wanted to protect the organization from demise. Honestly, I didn't know if we would survive, and there were very few positive indicators (particularly from my boss).

I thought I needed to project some sort of hope to our remaining staff. And that was certainly true. But I made the strategic and dishonest move of allowing a vision for the future to trump vulnerability and full-disclosure. I met multiple times with our remaining staff following the lay-offs (which, by the way, were made significantly worse as half of the lay-offs were immediate and half of them came with six months' notice—so we had a handful of walking dead employees in our midst during this transition when I was attempting to pump everyone up about our future). I briefly acknowledged the pain of the lay-offs, but emphasized our future. I didn't reveal my own struggle, and I mostly protected our corporate parent (which was, I suppose, my obligation). As a result, the remaining staff—not to mention the laid-off staff still in our midst—quickly lost trust in me. And when they lost trust, they had no interest in being a part of the rosy future I was trying to paint. Our amazing culture quickly evaporated and was replaced by silence, awkwardness, a lack of passion for our work, and a lack of willingness to collaborate.

THE ROLE OF TRUST

Trust is, perhaps, the single greatest factor in leadership. And, while trust is often lacking in hierarchical power structures (in churches or businesses), the funny thing is that it's one of the few facets described in this book that is possible within traditional hierarchical power structures (if you want a good book on this—trust in the context of traditional power structures, that is—I recommend Stephen M. R. Covey's *The Speed of Trust*).[18]

The reason trust is possible even in hierarchical systems boils down to this: Trust is 100% dependent on honesty. If a hierarchical power-based leader is fully honest and transparent (a rare occurrence, to be sure), it's possible to instill trust. But, more often than not, the mindset of a leader in utilizing role power and hierarchy has a mindset that says, "I know things you cannot and should not know; they are not your job to know them." If the leader were, somehow, able to be completely honest with herself (another rarity), the truth would be closer to, "Being less than transparent and fully honest with you protects my position of power, control, and authority over you. You are more dependent on me when I know more than you do."

Ah, but this tactic just doesn't work.

Trust is 100% possible to build. Here's the equation I've come up with for building trust:

$$\textbf{(Pure Intention + Action and Honesty)} \times \textbf{Time} = \textbf{Trust}$$

Of course, trust is very easy to lose (in a second).

It is also possible to rebuild trust after it's been lost. But the equation gets more complex:

$$\textbf{(Owning Up + Checking In + Pure Intention + Action and Honesty)} \times \textbf{Time}^2 = \textbf{Rebuilt Trust}$$

I have an axiom I teach in my youth worker coaching groups when we're talking about trust: *Without trust and safety, your ministry will not experience communion. And without communion, the ministry will be clubbish and wimpy.*

If you're my leader and I don't trust you:

- We will likely have friction (or at least be poised

for it).

- Small things will flash into big issues.

- I will resist collaboration.

- I will be skeptical of your leadership and motives.

- I will hoard information and resources.

- I will avoid engaging in the non-work relational glue that makes great teams.

- I will unconsciously believe bad rumors I hear about you and be skeptical of good rumors I hear about you.

- I will struggle to advocate for you.

- I will subconsciously (or even consciously) not contribute to the larger vision you are casting.

THE ROLE OF THE TRUST GUARD

If we want our organizational teams (and, again, this applies to volunteer teams as well as groups of employees) to experience wholeness and full embracing of the organizational mission, we have to place the value of alignment in a place of preeminence. In *Youth Ministry 3.0*, I wrote about the goal of "communion"— authentic community, with Christ in the mix.[19] Pulling the essence of that into a workplace or ministry team, organizations and teams can find missional alignment experienced in community by all members of the team.

The *Trust Guard* is passionate about these truths. This leader is vigilant in watching for actions, vibes, systems, and verbiage that threaten trust. And, this leader is vigilant in watching for actions, vibes, systems, and verbiage that build trust (highlighting these so others can reproduce them).

The *Trust Guard* is ruthless in protecting trust, is committed to honesty and transparency. This leader has a zero-tolerance attitude toward teasing and shaming. They chafe at, and are sometimes whistle-blowers about, organizational spin and leadership manipulation.

What if one of the primary ways we leaders exercise our power is by being honest?

A friend of mine was at the center of a recent mission board organizational blunder (a gross understatement) that has completely destroyed trust with many of their staff, donors, and other followers. This particular mission board received information, decades ago, about one of their missionary doctors perpetrating pedophilia on pre-teen and young teen missionary kids (of which my friend was one).[19] The mission board responded by covering it up. The issues were brought up at multiple points over the last 20-plus years; and each time, they promised action but took none.

Not only is the wrong perpetrated in this example horrific on many other levels, the result has been—as I've watched this unfolding in real time—a systemic and complete breakdown of trust. Trust in the organization and its leaders has been shot for a long time for those closest to the crime; but now that the story has come to light, trust has been eroded at levels that reach far and wide, including affiliated churches and donors.

Justice, in situations like this, gets more and more difficult without honesty.

I'm also reminded of one of the (rare?) times I think I got this right: when it was brought to our attention at Youth Specialties that we had published some blatantly racist content in one of our books, and we were called out by the Asian American church community.[20] In this case (as would have been true with the missions agency), it would have been better had we not allowed the offense to occur in the first place. But we screwed up; and the only right response was full disclosure, complete honesty, and swift action.

Now, you could say that this was all external and more about our interface with customers. But the impact on our staff was significant, and the way we handled it (both in how we talked about it internally and the steps our staff saw us taking) had an enormous impact on the level of trust internally. It was—counter-intuitively—one of those times when our screw-up resulted in more missional alignment (and communion) for our staff team.

So, back to the question at hand: What would it look like if, as a leader trying to lead without power, your primary expression of the power provided by your title or position were *the relentless pursuit of honesty*?

And, if you're in a role with positional power, are you willing to identify some *Trust Guards* and empower them to hold you accountable?

10
COLLABORATION GUIDE

The junior high pastor at my church recently graduated from the coaching program I lead and learned the process and power of developing ministry values. So, he asked me to help lead a collaborative process to that end.

In most ministry settings, that point person would have gone off on his own and written out some values, *possibly* vetting them past a couple people for input and attaboys. But Jarred wanted and needed collaboration. Most of our volunteer team retreated to a cabin in the mountains (coincidentally about a half mile from where I'm currently writing). We had a big meal together, laughed, and prayed; then Jarred set the stage for what we were about to do. Then he had me lead the group through the following collaborative exercises:

1. We opened with Blue Sky Dreaming, filling multiple sticky-note flip chart pages with responses to the question: "If resources and permission were unlimited, and we were guaranteed success, what would we want to do?" This collaborative exercise is very right-brained, creative, and serves two functions: It breaks past limited thinking right from the get-go, and it starts to reveal seeds of values.

2. After a break, we spent a chunk of time identifying a giant list of our current values (the "Meeting 1" step explained in the values discernment process in chapter five).

3. Then, we slept on it (which was thankfully not a collaborative exercise).

4. Next up was identifying the good and beautiful items from the list of current values ("Meeting 2" in chapter five). After a bit of discussion, we had everyone spend 30 minutes prayerfully looking over the list and asking God, "Which of these do we need to protect?" Then we did a version of casting lots: I gave each person three votes and told them they could use them on three separate values, all on one, or two and one. I reminded them that while this could look like a democratic vote, we were looking

for God's leading and praying that
God's dreams for us would be revealed through
this prayerful process.

5. Next, we repeated this process but focused on
   current values that were destructive ("Meeting
   3" in chapter five).

6. The resulting list of values were so clear and
   compelling that we hardly needed the final
   step of considering if anything "new" needed to
   be added to the list.

Then we let the list ferment for three or four months.
Our desire was that each of us would prayerfully
consider the list and ask for God's input—had we
gotten it right or not?

The next step in collaboration involved less people,
as we wanted to identify some strategic moves to lean
into the aspirational values. Jarred pulled together five
of us in my backyard on a lovely San Diego evening.
I talked to them about Key Leverage Points, strategic
actions that would have the greatest impact on moving
us toward embodiment of our values. We prayed and
had robust collaborative conversation, fairly quickly
agreeing on three initiatives that would help us move
toward embodiment of the two values that were the
most aspirational (in other words, the two values we
were currently not living into at all).

Another month later, Jarred and I met to come up with goals and action steps for those strategic choices, and there are now conversations and calendar items that reflect this process.

In case you didn't notice this in that story, Jarred was functioning as the *Collaboration Guide*, not me. I was invited *into* collaboration, as were a dozen other people.

In many ways, this is not a revolutionary story. Many of you reading this have been a part of similar processes. But honestly, I'm amazed how bad churches can be at collaboration, which is particularly striking since most of the "work" of any church is carried out by volunteers. In many church settings, what passes as collaboration is really just an authoritative, hierarchical leader (in a position of power) telling a group of volunteers what they need to do together and calling that collaboration.

IT'S COLLABORATION GUIDE, NOT COLLABORATION DICTATOR

Collaboration prioritizes a diversity of input, opinions, skills, and experiences over the singular strength of a powerful mind, or a powerful skill set, or a powerful position. Of course, collaboration *can* result in watered-down results, groupthink, or conflict. And that's why

122

great collaboration needs a *Collaboration Guide*.

The *Collaboration Guide* begins by understanding the benefits, risks, and processes of collaboration. Then this leader becomes invitational, encouraging people that their contribution will be valued. Guiding, and not dictating, this leader shepherds the process, ensuring that no one is pulling power plays and that everyone is both being heard and following through on their commitments.

If you're in a position of authority and trying to lead collaboratively, you must choose to forfeit power. You're not really guiding collaboration if you just get input from people and still make decisions and carry out the important work all by yourself.

Oh, and a *Collaboration Guide* understands that there's a difference between problems to be solved and tensions to be protected. I heard this point once in a talk given by Andy Stanley, and it has always stuck with me.[21] In any healthy collaborative process, tensions will naturally arise, as diverse humans will always bring opinions and perspectives to the table that are different from each other. Stanley suggested (and I agree) that, when tensions arise on a team, our natural inclination as a leader is to rush in with a solution—either a compromise or a selection of winner and loser. But not

123

all tensions are problems to be solved, and the *Collabo-ration Guide* intuitively understands this and uses self-discipline in parsing the difference. Some tensions are actually healthy and life-giving to a collaborative process, as long as those on either side of the tension are respectful to each other and remain open and curious.

I've teased out this idea already in this book, but my contention is that the best ministry leaders in our current cultural context have three skills (or, if they don't possess these skills, they have a commitment to surrounding themselves with others who do): spiritual discernment, contextualization insight and application, and a passion for hosting collaboration.

Collaboration is messy. It can be cumbersome. It can create political and relational tensions. But it is better in just about every way. Collaboration is a reflection of the various spiritual giftings the Apostle Paul writes about, a reflection of each person's *Imago Dei*, and a reflection of the priesthood of all believers.

And collaboration works at a practical level: Whatever hierarchical power a leader might forfeit by leading collaboratively is gained by an order of magnitude in terms of buy-in, shared ownership of mission, creativity, follow-through, quantity of output, breaking up groupthink, avoiding stupid errors and blind alleys, and all sorts of other CYA dead ends.

This is one of the biggest leadership lessons I've learned in the ministries I've been a part of: When we operated collaboratively, we kicked butt and had a blast doing it. When we chose to or were forced to operate in more traditional top-down decision-making modalities, the fun went away, the mission lost focus, and the ministry suffered.

A final challenge: Collaboration requires leading from within, not leading from out in front. Are you ready to make room for the potential messiness in order to experience new organizational vitality?

11
CONVICTION, COLLABORATION, AND CALLING: THE PIECE-PARTS OF 21ST-CENTURY MINISTRY LEADERSHIP

Leadership is changing. And this is a very, very good thing. Unfortunately, my observation is that approaches to leadership are changing in the business world far ahead of changes in church and ministry world. As often seems to be the case, we're behind; and this is particularly problematic when our theological convictions about leadership should have already brought us to a place of powerless leadership.

The era of the autocratic, top-down leader is on the way out. There will still be jerks and megalomaniacs who somehow end up overseeing others—in business and in the church. But that sort of leader is increasingly tolerated less—by all stakeholders and participants (employees, staff, volunteers, parishioners) who, not caring as much about institutional loyalty, are free to move on and find a healthier context.

At the conclusion of each cohort in our Youth Ministry Coaching Program, each participant writes Growth Affirmation and Challenge summaries for each of the participants. And I write these for each participant also, naming the amazing transformation I've seen in each of their lives over the year we've spent together. In the process of writing these, I am continually struck by how many churches are riddled with lousy leadership.

The good news is that a new kind of leader—one who leads without power—is on the rise.

Great leaders are anchored by three things: Conviction, Collaboration, and Calling.

Conviction isn't about being the sole vision caster.

It's not about forcing an agenda onto everyone.

It's not about being the heavy.

Conviction is about being a *Culture Evanglist* and *Mission Curator*.

Conviction is about ruthlessly protecting the values and not being swayed by attractive ideas (financial benefit, numerical-growth benefit, keeping the peace, pleasing the powerful) that erode the values.

Collaboration isn't about forced fun.

It's not about tokenism.

And it doesn't mean democracy.

Collaboration is about being a *Uniqueness DJ* and, obviously, a *Collaboration Guide*. Collaboration is about creating space and processes and an ecosystem that values meaningful input and offers active participation at every level.

And calling. Calling isn't about filling seats.

It's not about manipulation.

It's not about isolation.

Calling is about being a *Storytelling Host*, a *Champion of Hope*, and a *Trust Guard*.

Calling is about living into who you were made to be. It's the self-actualized leader, humble and open, rooted in a spiritual sense of urgency, committed to the mission and unwavering in a sense of movement. It's about living this and calling others to this greater purpose.

Conviction, collaboration, and calling. How are you living them out this week?

FINAL APPLICATION

Trust me on this: You cannot play all nine of these roles. You can *value* all of these roles, but you can't become the best person in your organization for every single one of them.

What you *can* do, though:

- Review the nine metaphorical job titles (you could use the Table of Contents for this purpose), and, as I suggested at the end of chapter one, notice:

  ▶ One or two "job titles" that you're already living into. Maybe you now have new language for something you were sort of doing, and maybe you're challenged to step it up. But it's likely that you noticed one (or two) of these frameworks that is already a part of your practice of leadership.

▶ Then, identify one or two "job titles" that you resonate with but aren't living into or exercising. When you read that chapter (or those chapters), the ideas connected with you at a deep level. Maybe you thought, "That is *totally* within my wheelhouse, and I need to start doing this!"

- For that last item (the one or two metaphorical job titles that you want to step into), take a moment to identify two or three action steps you can put into practice *this* week. Honestly, if you're anything like me, unless you start to take steps in this direction, your insights and new passion can quickly fade and be forgotten. Cement your new commitment with action.

- Finally, share these ideas with other leaders in your organization (church, ministry). If you're part of a leadership team (a church staff or the leadership team of a particular ministry), consider together which of you could step into which role or roles. How cool if you're able to find ownership and passion for all nine of them on a single leadership team.

May God bless you richly as you lean into a more Jesus-y style of leadership, and may that style of leadership build the church and expand the Kingdom of God, through you!

ENDNOTES

1. De Pree, Max. *Leading Without Power: Finding Hope in Serving Community* (San Francisco: Jossey-Bass, 2003).
2. Collins, Jim. *Good to Great: Why Some Companies Make the Leap... And Others Don't* (New York: HarperBusiness, 2001).
3. Here's a helpful Harvard Business Review article on Level 5 Leadership, written by Collins: http://hbr.org/hb-main/resources/pdfs/comm/microsoft/level-five.pdf.
4. Collins, 2001.
5. Philippians 2:6-8.
6. John 6:38.
7. Epstein, Robert. *Teen 2.0: Saving Our Children and Families from the Torment of Adolescence* (Fresno, CA: Quill Drive Books, 2010). See http://drrobertepstein.com/.
8. De Pree, p. 19-20.
9. Starbucks now offers recycling, though I don't presume it's because of Riley's pestering. But, maybe...?
10. Oestreicher, Mark. *Youth Ministry 3.0: A Manifesto of Where We've Been, Where We Are, and Where We Need to Go* (Grand Rapids: Zondervan, 2008).
11. See: https://www.zapposinsights.com/.
12. Some readers will note that this is close to Marshall McLuhan's famous sound bite, "The medium is the message." I would contend that the two statements are not the same and are addressing different issues.
13. Godin, Seth. *Purple Cow: Transform Your Business by Being Remarkable* (New York: Portfolio, 2003).
14. Oestreicher, Mark. *Hopecasting: Finding, Keeping and Sharing the Things Unseen* (Downers Grove, IL: Intervarsity Press, 2014).
15. De Pree, p. 149.

16. Meredith's husband eventually got appointed to a church in a different part of the state, and Meredith worked hard to help the ministry become self-sustaining before she left.
17. Wikipedia contributors. "Anthropology," *Wikipedia: The Free Encyclopedia* (website), November 15, 2016, https://en.wikipedia.org/wiki/Anthropology.
18. Covey, Stephen M. R. *Speed of Trust: The One Thing That Changes Everything* (New York: Free Press, 2006).
19. See: http://www.abwe.org/.
20. Oestreicher, Mark. "A Public Apology to Our Asian-American Brothers and Sisters," *WhyIsMarko* (blog), March 2, 2007, http://whyismarko.com/a-public-apology-to-our-asian-american-brothers-and-sisters/.
21. I have wracked my brain to try to remember where I heard Andy Stanley say this, but I don't exactly remember. My guess is that it was in one of the main session talks he gave through the years at the National Youth Workers Convention. Knowing Andy, I would expect the idea shows up somewhere in one of his excellent books also.